T0244813

Person Means Relation

Books of Interest from St. Augustine's Press

D. C. Schindler, *God and the City:*
An Essay in Political Metaphysics

Robert C. Koons, *Is St. Thomas's Aristotelian*
Philosophy of Nature Obsolete?

Kevin Hart, *Contemplation and Kingdom:*
Aquinas Reads Richard of St. Victor

Wayne J. Hankey, *Aquinas's Neoplatonism in*
the Summa Theologiae on God:
A Short Introduction

John F. Boyle, *Master Thomas Aquinas and the*
Fullness of Life

Robert J. Spitzer, S.J., *Evidence for God from*
Physics and Philosophy

Michael Franz (editor),
Eric Voegelin's Late Meditations and Essays:
Critical Commentary Companions

Charles P. Nemeth, *Aquinas on Crime*

Peter Kreeft, *Summa Philosophica*

Peter Kreeft, *The Platonic Tradition*

St. Anselm of Canterbury
(Matthew D. Walz, translator), *Proslogion*

Rémi Brague, *Anchors in the Heavens*

Roberto Regoli, *Beyond the Crises in the Church:*
The Pontificate of Benedict XVI

Person Means Relation
David Walsh
With a response by Matthew D. Walz,
and a reply by David Walsh

ST. AUGUSTINE'S PRESS
South Bend, Indiana

Copyright © 2024 by David Walsh
and Matthew D. Walz

All rights reserved. No part of this book may be
reproduced, stored in a retrieval system, or
transmitted, in any form or by any means,
electronic, mechanical, photocopying, recording, or
otherwise, without the prior permission of St.
Augustine's Press.

Manufactured in the United States of America.

paperback ISBN: 978-1-58731-673-9
ebook ISBN: 978-1-58731-674-6

1 2 3 4 5 6   29 28 27 26 25 24

**Library of Congress Control Number:
2024940222**

For more information about the University of
Dallas Aquinas Lectures, and a list of volumes
available for purchase from St. Augustine's Press,
see www.udallas.edu/aquinaslecture.

Table of Contents

NOTE

This volume is the fruit of the forty-first annual Aquinas Lecture at the University of Dallas, hosted by the Department of Philosophy and delivered by Prof. David Walsh on January 26, 2023. We thank Dr. Walsh once more for the opportunity to think along with him, in the spirit of St. Thomas. We thank as well our colleague Matthew Walz for his insightful contribution to this conversation, here published along with the lecture and followed by a response by Dr. Walsh.

Thanks are due also to our colleague Lance Simmons, for copy-editing the manuscripts; our staff colleague Sarah Oates, for her beautiful new cover design for the series; and Benjamin Fingerhut of St. Augustine's Press, for his hard work and friendly professionalism.

Together with Dr. Walsh, we dedicate this volume to distinguished professor emeritus of philosophy William A. Frank, whose work on personalism and Catholic social thought brought Dr. Walsh to our campus; to Bill's wife, Therese; and to the late Bruce Fingerhut, founder of St. Augustine's Press, who first agreed to publish these lectures.

Faculty of the Department of Philosophy,
University of Dallas
Memorial of St. Anselm
April 21, 2024

Person Means Relation
St. Thomas Aquinas Lecture
University of Dallas, January 26, 2023
David Walsh

When we think about persons we often seem to have started on the wrong foot. In a world of things it is easy to overlook what it means to be a person. But then we have made a monstrous mistake. We must not treat persons as things for they are entirely different. The problem is that our language is dominated by things that have existence, while persons seem to emerge from beyond existence. They carry their existence within them as what it means to be a person. That is why they are sacrosanct.

A zone of inviolability surrounds them, even if we cannot explain whence it derives. They have transcended who they are before they have even arrived. That is why they must not be abused or killed as if it means nothing. We too are touched by the inwardness that seems to pervade their reality. They have an inside we intuit immediately. Yet we have no word for that non-present presence. The best we have been able to say is that they hold a mask, *prósōpon*, a face before us as the way they conceal what is not and perhaps cannot be revealed. It is from this Greek term *prósōpon* that we get the name person and from the Latin *personare* the parallel notion of a mask that is sounded through. In neither case do we have a technical term, and that shortcoming has marked the whole tradition up to modern times. It is arguable that it was only the necessity of distinguishing between the three persons of the Trinity, as well as the two natures in the person of Christ, that compelled Christian theologians to hammer out some vague sense of what it means to be a person. This is despite the ubiquity of persons as the most evident aspect of what each of us is and of the world of our interactions with one another.

We never get away from persons, who are so close to us that we scarcely possess a language to navigate the reality of persons. How could we forget what we have always already forgotten? In what follows I will sketch an attempt to find a more adequate way of speaking that saves us from defaulting to the language of things. We begin with St. Thomas, whose own struggle with the question has given us the title of our talk, without necessarily fully explaining what is involved. A wider application of his striking insight would have to await a language of inwardness that was not readily available to him. To develop it, relation would, second, have to be understood as a holding of the other inwardly. This is made possible by the modern idea of self-determination as, third, the distinctive mark of what it means to be a person. Holding existence in our own hands we become capable of giving ourselves to others and receiving others within us.

Meeting outside of the whole, each is, in the formulation of Immanuel Kant, a whole or an end-in-himself-or-herself. Finally we glimpse self-transcendence as mutuality, the possibility of communication between persons that Thomas had identified as relation. A very different notion of the person as transcendence begins to suggest why his reflection centered on the relation between the persons of the Trinity. What it means to be a person is so far above our ordinary mode of discourse that it begins, not surprisingly, with an admission of our philosophical incapacity.

Person as relation

Even when Alcibiades ruptured the tranquility of the *Symposium* and gave his drunken panegyric to the person of Socrates, we only catch a glimpse of the kind of impact he referenced (215b–222c). The pain of that fractured relationship, portending the fracture of Athenian power, is displayed but never explicated. Inwardness is everywhere in that painful confession, including the call of inwardness that is refused, to such an extent that we seem to be on the brink of acknowledging the centrality of the impact of persons on one another. Yet it recedes. The intensity of the personal touch, never more palpable than in a dialogue on love, is discreetly covered behind layers of irony that seem to unfold endlessly. When Aristotle resumes his cooler discussion of *philia*, friendship, it is within the context of a work on character, that is, on ethics, that requires a sensitive reading to discern the personal and interpersonal depths that lie behind it. The friend may indeed be "another self," but what does it mean to have that capacity to live within one another? Only his own singular admission of *sunaisthesis*, joint perception, opens the door to that very different vista from the work on self that is the main topic of the *Ethics*. Nowhere is there a hint of awareness that philosophy might require a very different path of reflection to follow out its implications. The time for the differentiation of the person was not yet there. Or we might say, it was not opportune because the historical setting had not yet made it imperative. Without a pressing necessity, *prósōpon* could remain a term of casual use for actors on the stage rather than a technical term for what most defines us. It would not be until the Church Fathers had a problem of sufficient gravity that they would have to hammer out what it means to be a person. Faith in the three persons within the one God and the two natures within one person, was that unmistakable necessity.[1] The only problem was that once the immediate urgency of dogmatic clarification had been surmounted, the wider implications for the notion of the person, especially its application to all persons, could again fall by the philosophical wayside.

Perhaps there was no better indication of this postponement than the definition of the person, minted by Boethius (480–524) and transmitted to the succeeding centuries, for it was just the kind of formula—"a person is a substance of a rational nature"—that blocked the path to further development.[2] Gone was

1   Colin Patterson, *Chalcedonian Personalism: Rethinking the Human* (Oxford: Peter Lang, 2016).
2   Boethius, *Contra Eutychen*, sections 2–4.

the opportunity for a richer and more supple understanding that might navigate what it means to be a person. Even Augustine's formidable exploration of interiority in the *Confessions* was not enough to spur further reflection. His own account of the Trinity would remain solidly within the boundaries of a substance-driven metaphysics that fell disappointingly short of the mutuality of persons it seemed to promise. Faculty psychology was firmly on its way to supplanting a psychology of persons in their unboundedness. This was probably why the formula of Boethius prevailed with such solidity into the medieval period and beyond. "A person is a substance of a rational nature" became the outermost boundary of thought, even as its shortcomings as a paradigm mounted continually. The deference of the medieval mind, its fidelity to the reconciliation of sources that persist in their tension, is amply on display in their struggles with the notion of the person. Not surprisingly, the work of the greatest medieval mind, the remarkable synthetic genius of Thomas Aquinas, epitomizes the strengths and weaknesses most clearly. While taking note of them we should also remind ourselves that, outside of the realm of philosophical and theological reflection, a flexible understanding of the person marched in unbroken continuity within the legal tradition that had always known its practical indispensability. As the unique bearer of responsibility before the law, the person could not be submerged in any amorphous generality. Each person is a unique "I."[3]

For St. Thomas, however, the problem was not that the richness of legal practice, canonist or jurist, had eluded him, but rather that he held steadfastly to the authoritative definition handed on to him. The formulation of Boethius had acquired an immovability he was loathe to challenge. Perhaps this was a factor that deterred him from expanding his remarkably subtle analysis of persons, developed largely within his theology of the Trinity, to a wider account of persons that might include all rational beings. Whatever the reason,

3 John Finnis, "The Priority of Persons," *Intention and Identity* (Oxford: Oxford University Press, 2011), 19–35.

it is fascinating to see him grapple with the confines of a definition whose limitations became increasingly evident. As always, he retained a respectful silence rather than disclose his own speculative daring. Yet the struggle itself powerfully speaks to the inflexibility of the Boethian formula, especially in the hands of one deeply reluctant to overturn it. Paradigm shifts, we are reminded, are not always announced by the innovators, for the difficulty of maintaining a paradigm, in the face of contrary evidence, can speak just as loudly. At any rate such shifts are rarely intended but emerge as an incidental consequence of more deeply probing the confusions history has bequeathed to us. Like most of the medieval monks, Thomas did not set out to change or conserve a tradition, or to build Christendom, but only to find God. It was to understand better who had called him that he took up the task of reflecting on what it means to be a person. Thus it is almost by accident that he blurts out two of the most astonishing pronouncements concerning what it means to be a person.

The first is that personhood is the reality of God. "I answer that, Person signifies what is most perfect in all nature—that is, a subsistent individual of a rational nature. Hence, since everything that is perfect must be attributed to God; because His essence contains every perfection, this name person is fittingly applied to God; not however as it is applied to creatures, but in a more excellent way" (*ST* I, q. 29, a. 3). What is striking here is that being or subsistence is no longer the highest, but personhood is that apex of reality. However it is conceived, God is not simply the highest being; rather, person is the highest being, with all of the mysterious dynamic of self-giving, of love, embedded in that term. Substance is what endures in being, what supports accidents, a *suppositum*. A person is always engaged in the communication of its being. A substance preserves itself, whereas a person pours himself or herself out. The pre-eminence of God does not consist in self-subsistence but in self-giving. Already the Boethian paradigm has begun to shift, for the accent is no longer on substance but on what substance does, even without limit. It is perhaps not too much of a stretch to suggest that it was Thomas's decision to begin with what it means to be a person, the person of God, that led him toward the unfolding of the Trinity of persons that is God. Substance suggests what can be alone, person indicates what cannot be except in relation to another person.

This is the second and most daring idea that his meditation uncovers, especially once he begins with personhood as the being of God. He asks whether the word "person" signifies relation. Thomas proceeds cautiously by invoking the Boethian definition, in which distinct persons, distinct substances, may or may not enter into relations with one another. But what about God? Relation in God cannot be an accident in a subject, but must be in the divine essence itself as subsisting. "Therefore a divine person signifies a relation as subsisting." To be God the Father is not an accidental relationship, but who God is. Relations that for all others would be accidental to their substance are in God the essence of what it means to be God. In this way Thomas deftly enlarges the meaning of personhood along a path of analogy that begins, not with finite persons, but with infinite persons, as the model. It is only later, perhaps much later, after we have become fathers, that we catch a glimpse of that mysterious enlargement of who we are as earthly fathers. We have not acquired children, rather children have acquired us, and reveal the un-renounceable truth of who we are. Of course we may still be reading into it more than the text can bear, but it is hard to resist the suggestion that this is what Thomas intends by his delicate dislodgement of the Boethian primacy of substance. "Thus it is true to say that the name person signifies relation directly, and the essence indirectly; not however, the relation as such, but as expressed by way of a *hypostasis* . . . and thus relation, as such, enters into the notion of the person indirectly." At that point he seems to be generalizing beyond the application of the term "relation" to the persons of the Trinity, and seems to be claiming it for wider application to all persons. The word "person" came to suggest relation, he hints, "so that this word person means relation not only by use and custom . . . but also by force of its own signification." (q. 29, a. 4).

The transformation of Western metaphysics, for which Joseph Ratzinger called, seems to be on the horizon within Thomas's silent overturning of the paradigm of substance that ushers in a new paradigm of the person.[4] The difficulty that he and we have

---

4 Speaking of Augustine's effort to hold together the ideas of substance and relation, Ratzinger allows himself a more paradigm-shifting thought. "Therein lies concealed a revolution in man's view of the world: the sole dominion of thinking in terms of substance is ended; relation is discovered as an equally valid primordial mode of reality. It becomes possible to surmount what we call today 'objectifying thought'; a new plane of being comes into view." *Introduction to Christianity*, trans. J. R. Foster and Michael J. Miller (San Francisco: Ignatius, 2004; original, 1968), 184. For Ratzinger's surprisingly critical assessment of the failure of the tradition to enlarge on this beginning see "Retrieving the Tradition: Concerning the notion of person in Theology," *Communio* (Fall 1990), 439–54. His own effort at restoring the centrality of the person is ongoing but culminates in the encyclicals of his pontificate, as I have tried to explain in "The Person as

is that we lack a means of visualizing what it means to be the kind of being that gives its being away. What does it mean to put the other in place of the self? How is it possible to be selfless without a self? Nothing in the model of things that cling to their existence can furnish a similitude. We realize that a model of existence built on the enduring presence of things overlooks that which has always escaped merely finite presence. This is why Thomas's succinct remarks about the meaning of person within the Trinity are so momentous, even without his elaboration of their consequences for a philosophy of the person more broadly. Substance is no longer the model when it has been displaced by the primacy of the person. It is from the person that we draw a notion of substance that is no longer tied to its hold on being. To be a person is to be like God, who could hold onto his being but out of love continually

the Opening to the Secular World: Benedict and Francis," Walsh, *The Priority of the Person* (Notre Dame: University of Notre Dame Press, 2020), Ch. 14.

dispenses it. We are the image of God, not in being a rational substance, but in being the substance that transcends itself. Instead of remaining at the level of an external definition, the application of genus and species to a world of things, we have reached the inner reality that sustains what the definition simply describes from the outside. If the person is the highest reality, there is no model of it beyond the highest perfection of personhood. There is no way of understanding the higher in terms of the lower, for no matter how strongly material existence has a grip on us, it can never yield a path to what lies beyond it. The selfish gene cannot explain the unselfish gene, nor the mind that aims at understanding it. Person is a *sui generis* reality that has no exemplar but God. The end of a metaphysics of presence is palpable when it opens upon that which makes all presence possible.

We still lack a model of how it is possible to cling to being while continually transcending it. In the scale of all finite measurement we cannot give of ourselves without diminution, but that is the reality of all that is personal. By sharing knowledge I do not possess less knowledge; by sharing myself I do not become less of a self. Aristotle glimpsed this when he tried to explain that the friend who expended his money on behalf of his friend gained more than his friend received. Only in a world of persons does it make sense to say that you become more by becoming less. That is the significance of Thomas's other great principle of the person as relation. It fixes in our minds how it is possible to be a person that continually pours itself out without loss, contrary to the logic of all immanent being. The reason the person is the highest reality in being is that it continually surpasses mere being. It *is* in an utterly different mode of being that has no similitude beyond itself. The person is by way of self-giving. It *is* in the mode of non-being, so that nothing in being can assail it. It shares in the life of God. Self-giving is the life of God, and this is why there must be otherness in God. The Trinity of persons in God is something we discern most clearly through the revelation that invites us to participate in the life of the Trinity. But we recognize it as something we might even be able to glimpse outside of that dispensation. It is in the logic of what it means to be a person that loss is gain, an experience that overwhelms every young mother with the astonishment of being the first to discover it. Thomas provides a comparably striking formulation in his assertion that the word "person" signifies relation. Of course we human persons never manage to set aside our separate substances, but only glimpse it at that boundary moment when our existence is wholly defined by the other. In his analysis of the persons of the Trinity Thomas was able to affirm it as the paradigm for relation as to who they are. "Therefore a divine person signifies a relation as subsisting."

To grasp the full weight of that extraordinary statement, we must begin to appreciate the extent to which it has displaced the language of *hypostasis* / substance in speaking of the Trinity. This may have been the point where person as relation overturns the notion of person as substance. Or it may be more accurate to suggest that the model of substance has been surpassed by the model of person. That which gives itself away exceeds that which maintains itself in being. It is the more eminent reality that has no analogue but the life of God, that we see in the complete sharing of self within the persons of the Trinity. Nothing immanent or natural compares to it. One wonders whether Thomas's stunning admission that all he had written is "straw" was not prompted by such a glimpse of the communion between the persons of the Trinity. Could it be that his inability to break free from the constraints of a language of fixed substance, to really embrace the personalist revolution toward which his thought pointed, provoked this poignant admission? Not all mystics lapse into silence. Many become even more voluble as they seek to make language convey what is beyond language. But that would be to fully embrace the discourse of persons who always say more than they can say. The concision of scholastic distinctions hardly lent itself to such overflowing, even when its trace is palpably evident. To do so would have required a fuller embrace of Thomas's other remarkable assertion that the person is the highest reality there is. If that is the case, then discourse about persons must remain consistent with that realization. It cannot remain an account of persons that excludes the one to whom it is addressed. Person always means relation. Someone is utterly different from something.[5]

Relation as inwardness

The only way persons can be known is personally. Over and above all that is said and done is the person. Each person is a moment of transcendence within a finite world that can only be known as such. Unique and irreplaceable, they can be known only in

5 This is an echo of Robert Spaemann's great work, *Persons: The Difference between "Someone" and "Something,"* trans. Oliver O'Donovan (Oxford: Oxford University Press, 1996). My own attempt to explicate this crucial distinction, especially with a view to the personalist approach, is in *Politics of the Person as the Politics of Being* (Notre Dame: University of Notre Dame Press, 2016).

themselves, not in anything else. The shift toward a language of persons who can be known only in their mutuality would await philosophical developments that were beyond the scholastic horizon. St. Thomas's achievement was that he accomplished so much within the limitations of what was available. It is in this sense not so surprising that it was only when he came to think through the inner relations between the persons of the Trinity that he touched on the interiority that characterizes all persons. Despite the extent to which Thomas's own life had been lived within that interior horizon, it eluded the capacity of his philosophical vocabulary to articulate the inwardness of its source. Only when we are reminded of this, for example by Andrew Pinsent, can we appreciate the second-person perspective that is the comprehensive setting for his ethics.[6] When we follow this fascinating suggestion we begin to gain clarity on matters that a more conventionally external reading

6   Andrew Pinsent, *The Second Person Perspective in Aquinas's Ethics* (New York: Routledge, 2012).

overlooks. Such notorious problems as whether Thomas could render a satisfactory account of natural virtue, and whether it could stand apart from the life of grace, only then begin to fall away. They cease to be problems once we admit that the life of nature is properly seen within the divine relationship. We are perhaps not far from the overarching insistence of Kierkegaard that the life of the person exists only within the God relation. The process of developing that more existential framework eluded the scholastics, even as they lived it out. Yet it would become the fruit of the modern turn toward existence, one that promised a new underpinning of faith once it could no longer be conceived in any external forms.

A new opening to faith as interiority would simultaneously disclose the horizon of the person and displace essentialist modes of thought.[7] The discovery of the person as the one who carries his or her existence, who ex-

7   St. Teresa of Avila, *The Interior Castle* (1588), finds surprising echoes in Descartes's *Meditations*.

ists in self-determination, is largely modern. Self-responsibility, even as the way responsibility toward others is configured, has always marked human life. What was not always available were the linguistic means of saying it, or of grasping the process of self-determination as what uniquely constitutes the person. Once again we recall that this perspective remained within the realm of law, in which everything hinges on the inner intention of persons. What is distinctive in the modern turn is that philosophy now explicitly embraces inwardness as its own starting point. This is why the interior perspective is so decisive, for it is in inwardness that each person takes possession of who they are and opens a process of self-disclosure and self-enactment with others. The person, who had for so long been casually identified with the mask, now steps forward as its bearer. But of course there is nothing to see beyond the self-presentation that has been made. The person remains invisible even to himself or herself. Inwardness is an elusive medium. A far more radical willingness to dwell with the uncertainty of disclosure, to recognize it as indispensable to the *sui generis* reality of the person, is the only way to secure what can be secured in this inescapably fluid process. The person *is* in himself or herself. Nothing can displace the one who addresses nor the one who is addressed. They meet in the mutuality of what is over and above all that is said and done, in a manner that can neither be doubted nor deflected. Call and response endure without substitution. It is as the bearer of responsibility that the person pre-eminently comes to light. The one who shares in that primordial freedom of self-creation has already stepped outside of time. Nothing finite can anchor those who have transcended all such limits.[8]

8   Václav Havel imagines himself awaiting a final judgment outside of time. "But why does this final evaluation matter so much to me? After all, at that point I shouldn't care. But I do care because I'm convinced that my existence—like everything else that has ever happened—has ruffled the surface of Being, and that after my little ripple, however marginal, insignificant, and ephemeral it may have been, Being is and always will be different from what it was before. All my life I have simply believed that

They may not be able to give themselves as completely as the persons of the Trinity in their mutual transparence, but human persons can give the tokens that betoken mutual self-giving. Each can set itself aside for the sake of the other and, in doing so, know the other as a person, that is, as a bearer of inwardness. It is striking that the demand to abolish legal slavery really gets underway at the same time as this heightened awareness of the person within the Enlightenment.[9] Without requiring extended argument, it emerges in a visceral revulsion against something no longer tolerable. We cannot look on one another as things that can be bought and sold with indifference, or with that minimal awareness that averts our eyes from the greatest crimes against humanity. Cruelty is

what is once done can never be undone and that, in fact, everything remains forever. In short, Being has a memory." *To the Castle and Back*, trans. Paul Wilson (New York: Knopf, 2006), 330.

9   Hans Joas, *The Sacredness of the Person: A New Genealogy of Human Rights* (Washington, DC: Georgetown University Press, 2013).

impossible when we look on the face of the other as the face of inwardness. This does not mean that we have always lived up to the high demand of gazing on the other as other, but we have at least become aware of why it has become so difficult to kill him or her. A hefty dose of ideology has always been required to make us forget what we cannot so easily forget, and that too has not exactly been in short supply in our modern world. The "power of the powerless," in Václav Havel's memorable phrase, has always been the capacity of reminding us that each one is a unique center of responsibility in the whole universe. In the striking formulation of Immanuel Kant, in legislating for themselves they legislate on behalf of all others.

Contrary to the conventional reading of Kant's moral philosophy as individualist, we begin to see that we cannot say "I" without including "you." Autonomy does not mean self-legislating in accord with one's own desires, irrespective of the rights and interests of others, for self-determination includes all others. It is a misinterpretation of Kant to think that his thought arises from the isolated ego, for the categorical imperative enjoins us to act in such a way that we can at the same time will that our actions should become universal law. We must act, not with a view to our private perspective, but with full regard to the perspective of others. It is almost as if he counsels us to think of the moral law in relation to others, as its prime directive. It is a moral philosophy that tests itself within the minds of others. Relation is there from the very beginning. "Do unto others as you would have them do unto you" is an injunction of great weight and authority, especially as it comes from Christ. But it does not unfold the why embedded within it. For that we must understand what it means to be a person in mutual openness to others. In an important sense persons are already in relation to others before they are in relation to themselves, although it is through that relationship to others that they gain a sense of who they are as selves.[10] This is why for Kant

10   Immanuel Levinas, *Totality and Infinity*, trans. Alphonso Lingis (Pittsburgh: Duquesne University Press, 1987).

the first formulation of the categorical imperative yields multiple equivalents that move successively in the direction of the impossibility of being persons outside of communion with others. Relation is not a mere aspiration, but rather the reality of who persons are, irrespective of whether they live up to its high calling.

The dignity of persons, Kant seems to say, lies in their capacity to recognize one another as persons. That is, in their capacity to grasp that they must always regard one another as ends-in-themselves and never as a mere means. As beings who can set themselves aside for the sake of fulfilling their duty, they bear existence within themselves in such a way that they surpass all that merely is. Each one is a new beginning that appears to come from beyond all that is solidly present in space and time. The language of substance is unsuited to beings who are capable of setting aside their substance for the sake of what is right. When Kant thinks about what makes such a condition possible, his reflections trail off into the reverential awe the thought inspires in him.

Without really voicing it he clearly implies
that persons participate in the primordial
dignity of that which is the highest divine reality. This is why the famous postulates of
God, freedom, and immortality play such an
important role in his moral philosophy, although they can have no basis within his
speculative thought. Once again it is capacity
for relation, for complete self-giving, that
marks the person who exists nowhere but in
that movement itself. Obviously without invoking St. Thomas, Kant is pointing toward
the mode of what it means to be a person
that is glimpsed in the account of the Trinity
of Persons.

Even when he thinks of the kind of association formed by persons who regard one another as ends-in-themselves, it is notable that
Kant introduces the formula of the "kingdom-
of-ends." Each regards the other as an end-in-
himself and thereby establishes an order that
revolves around the singularity of each one.
It is often overlooked, even by admirers of
Kant like John Rawls, the extent to which he
provides the most profound version of what
a liberal order, derived from the mutual and

reciprocal recognition of persons as persons, would look like. The readiness of each to set him or herself aside for the sake of the other is surely the endpoint of the notion of the person as relation. Who knew that the Trinity is the perfect exemplar of a liberal society?[11] The reference to a "kingdom" seems to lift it out of the realm of any mundane model of rule. What is decisive is that persons in Kant, and arguably in the modern account, are known less in terms of a definition that would derive from substance or nature, than in terms of the actions by which they become who they are. Persons *are* in the process of becoming persons. It is in their transcendence of all they have said and done, as the unending source of their own reality, that we perceive what it

11 His famous remark that "the problem of setting up a state can be solved even by a nation of devils (so long as they possess understanding)" highlights exactly what devils lack. Natural instincts are surpassed by the order of freedom that utterly transcends nature. See "Perpetual Peace" in *Political Writings*, ed. Hans Reiss (Cambridge: Cambridge University Press, 1970), 112.

means to be a person. The flash of transcendence that each of them is, a formulation that while not exactly found in Kant, is close to his assertion that they act from a standpoint outside of time.[12] In every respect he is the real exponent of the modern emphasis on the dignity of persons that reaches from the Book of Genesis notion of the imago Dei, to Thomas's affirmation of person as relation, to his own acknowledgment of each as an end-in-him or -herself.

Inwardness as transcendence of existence

Despite the clarity he had gained on the person as a relational process, Kant could not completely escape the suggestion that persons still exist in the mode of substances within the world. It was the modern concept of history, as an inexorable march of progress,

12 As a free moral being man "eventually views his existence *insofar as it does not stand under the conditions of time.*" *Critique of Practical Reason*, 97.

that forced him to see the jeopardy to which
their readiness to sacrifice themselves had ex-
posed them. To his credit Kant did nothing to
disguise or evade the jarring impact of this
realization upon him. As a child of the Enlightenment he could not abandon the self-
understanding of an age rooted in the
progress of science and the increasingly rational unfolding of life around him. But what
would this mean for persons who could perceive and admire the advance of history precisely because they could never be
completely subsumed within it? If each of
them existed merely to play a part in a wider
whole whose goal lay beyond them, what
would become of the equally stringent requirement that they be regarded as ends-in-
themselves and never a mere means toward
something else? The clash generated a shock-
ing sense of "disconcertment" (*befremendend*)
that Kant could neither shake nor suppress.[13]
His conviction of the inextinguishable dignity

13   "Idea for a Universal History with a Cosmopol-
     itan Purpose," Third Proposition, in *Political
     Writings*, 44.

of every single person saved him from the tendency toward instrumentalization, but he could not find a way of combining the movement of history with the transcendence of every person within it. The grip of the model of what maintains its hold on being was simply too strong to reach the model of that whose being consists in losing it. In the end the only model of the person is Jesus Christ and those who find their substance on the far side of loss.

It is by thinking through the logic of relation that a way may be found out of the conundrum that stopped Kant in his tracks. How is it possible to be a means that escapes the fate of being a mere means? How does one save one's life by losing it? The question has had a long historical unfolding without unpacking the cryptic insight contained within it. The paradigm of loss as gain can only be accessed in the reality of the person who has never been defined by gain or loss. Coming from before existence, the transcendence of it is already embedded in personhood. This is the complete self-giving toward which Thomas's notion of relation points.

The person has never ceased to give itself away. It is what we continually look for in communication with one another, and know as the touchstone of all genuine meeting between persons. Have we said what cannot be said, yet must be said, in giving ourselves? It is what all great speakers succeed in doing and even poor ones manage on occasion, when they say more than they were able to say. Run-of-the mill homilists and professors take comfort in the knowledge that their listeners have shown up, not because they are the most scintillating of communicators, but simply because they are themselves. The chance to hear the message from a live person always outweighs the content of a canned PowerPoint. The excess that is there in any genuine meeting is the excess of persons who know one another as unique and singular persons existing nowhere but in themselves. The problem that stumped Kant was that he regarded history as outside the persons whose actions constitute history. His conviction of the inextinguishable dignity of every single person saved him from the tendency toward instrumentalization, but he could not find a way of combining the progress of history with the transcendence of every person within it.

Such a combination would require recognition of the non-reducibility of every historical actor to his or her role within the process as a whole. Each would have to be seen as tied to an absolute utterly beyond the finitude of space-time boundaries. Kant's principle that persons must be regarded as ends-in-themselves and never as a mere means to some other goal would have to be fully embraced. He would have to admit that the objectifying view of history suggests the instrumentalization of everyone within it. To his credit, Kant admitted the shudder he felt at the prospect of dehumanization in that perspective. He knew enough to resist the totalitarian shadow that falls on all progressive narratives. But he could not find a way to recognize the condition of possibility of the historiographic enterprise as such. A little reflection, however, discloses the artificiality of the external viewpoint of history as a series of spectacles, leading to the superior viewpoint of the historian in the present. That viewpoint overlooks the realization that the narrator's present will be overtaken by a future for whom he too will have become a past to be regarded as a mere stepping-stone to the present. The illusion that each spectator within history possesses an unsurpassable viewpoint can be broken only if we recognize that the entire problem is possible only because we are never simply beings within history. Instrumentalization can be glimpsed because we are always more than instruments. We can ask about history only because we are never simply reducible to our role within it. Reflection on the meaning of history *is* our transcendence of history. We can question the goal or end of history because we always already stand beyond it. The person is the apocalypse of history. We can set ourselves aside for the sake of knowing and measuring everything and everyone we encounter. The problem with grand historical narratives is that they sweep up even those who are enacting and remembering the process. A remedy is available if we recall that historiography turns on the exclusion of historiographers from its account.

It is by leaving room for history that we can contemplate it. Even the suggestion that there is an end or a culmination of history, whether within time or beyond it, is intelligible only to persons who can set themselves apart from it all. There is no point at which those who recount history can be absorbed within it. But this also means that those who create history through their lives are also centers of transcendence within it. From whatever vantage we consider it, history has been surpassed by those who live it *and* by those who contemplate it. There is thus no goal of history that could supersede the persons who bear it as their destiny. There is no laurel that we the spectators or witnesses could bestow on those who have poured themselves out. This is the secret of the viewpoint of Lincoln's Gettysburg Address, as it is of all appropriate historical remembrance. We do not merely honor our benefactors or measure their contributions, for we revere them as immeasurable. Whatever they have given, they have given their all. It is in that sense that every person transcends the historical moment through which he or she passes. Even the calculation of the significance of their accomplishments exceeds any purely mundane measure that might be assigned to them. Having given the full measure of devotion, they have given the immeasurable. It is for this reason that we do not live within history as a finite realm of work and struggle, a realm that perennially falls short of the infinite promise it always seems to hold. The artificiality of such historical judgments must ultimately be set aside as incompatible with the immeasurability behind them. Within the finitude of historical events the infinity of every person lies hidden. It is only occasionally that the flash of transcendence renders that infinity perceptible, when persons give more than they can. They give themselves and, in this, they give the all that lifts them definitively beyond the limits of mundane existence.[14] All of this is

14 The transcendent finality of love is very well explored by Dietrich von Hildebrand in his account of the fulfillment of natural love in Christian *caritas*. *The Nature of Love*, trans. John F. Crosby with John Henry Crosby (South Bend, IN: St. Augustine's Press, 2009), ch. 11, "Caritas."

dimly intuited in Kant's conscientious struggle against the instrumentalization of the person within the idea of progress. It was impossible, he knew, because he had already reached the realization that each one is the end of history.

The most he could say is that together persons constitute a kingdom-of-ends, or ends-in-themselves. Within that phrase we catch a glimpse of the field of mutuality opened within history. It is not merely that each one possesses inwardness but that each thereby becomes an unsurpassable center of meaning and value within the whole. Even the self-consciousness that each possesses is not the final dimension of their existence, for the one who possesses it lies beyond it. This is the meaning of what it is to be a person. To identify the person as an end-in-himself-or-herself is to acknowledge the kind of being that each one is. Self-determination is only the most manifest expression of what the person is. It was for this reason that Kant made self-determination, autonomy, the centerpiece of his moral philosophy. But behind it lay a metaphysical opening to which Kant barely alluded. That is, that persons not only possess autonomy and ought to be so recognized by others, but that they exemplify the kind of being that can give or withhold itself as a whole. The awesome character of that reality did powerfully impress Kant as he marveled at the way persons can set aside all that makes them happy for the sake of doing what is right. How is a person like Franz Jägerstätter possible? He was the one Austrian who refused to serve in Hitler's army, knowing that it would bring about his certain execution.[15] Nothing was accomplished, as the lawyers and pastors told him. Yet he persevered on the side of what is right rather than become complicit in evil. Franz held his existence in his hands, as his response in the moment of truth made clear. In some

15 The recent movie by Terence Malick, *A Hidden Life*, has made the witness of Franz Jägerstätter far more widely known than it had been, even though he was beatified by Benedict XVI in 2007. Franz Jägerstätter, *Letters and Writings from Prison*, ed. Erna Putz, trans. Robert A. Krieg (Maryknoll, NY: Orbis, 2009). See also https://ihe.catholic.edu/my-big-discovery/

respects of course he held far more than the fate of his own soul, for in that decision his actions silently took responsibility for a whole society, perhaps the human race. Each of us, Terence Malick seems to emphasize, in the quotation from George Eliot that ends the movie about it is responsible for the sum total of good and evil in the universe.[16] Every person lives a hidden life, one that is largely invisible to others, but one that bears responsibility to all others in the web of relations that is far from invisible. Far from being merely centers of consciousness or experience, persons take their stand on realities that outweigh the whole cosmos.

This is why each person is unique and uniquely irreplaceable. What we remember about each person we meet and get to know is not what is visible on the outside, nor even

16   It is a quotation from the end of George Eliot's *Middlemarch*: "for the growing good of the world is partly dependent on unhistoric acts; and that things are not so ill with you and me as they might have been, is half owing to the number who lived faithfully a hidden life, and rest in unvisited tombs."

what they said or how they made us feel. All
of that is fleeting, and we shrug it off as the
mere surface through which we navigate our
lives together. What matters is the person in
himself or herself, utterly non-exchangeable
with any other. This is the substantive reality
we know in knowing a person. It is why we
strain to meet one another, knowing that in
every meeting there is an excess that cannot
be contained in any medium of exchange.
We might be inclined to think of this as the
inner reality of the person that somehow we
might reach by peeling back the successive
layers around it. But this too is a mistake
since even consideration of the person himself or herself cannot reach the innermost
self. There is only the person who has already demonstrated the capacity to step outside the self to contemplate and discuss the
distance. In the end we have to admit that we
are not in the realm of self-contained entities,
the world of things. Persons are a *sui generis*
reality without analogue in the objects with
which we are familiar. This has been the big
obstacle to understanding persons, souls,
and spirits. They are not things, because they

are ever ready to set aside the thing-like hold on existence in order to yield place to the other. It is because they are wholes that they can reach out to contain the whole. A society of persons is, in the words of Maritain, "a whole of wholes."[17] Only God seems to provide a suitable model of what the person is, but that is to get ahead of ourselves. For the moment it is enough to acknowledge that the enduring reality of persons is already accessible in the ordinary experience of persons we know and love. We know each one as a world in himself or herself.

That is why the person takes such priority over all else in the universe. Nothing and no one can take a person's place. It is as if there is a new birth of the universe in each case. The person exceeds all else because in a certain sense that is our experience of the astonishing big bang each one is.[18] They

17 *The Person and the Common Good* (Notre Dame: University of Notre Dame Press, 1966), 57.

18 Brendan Purcell, *From Big Bang to Big Mystery: Human Origins in Light of Creation and Evolution* (Hyde Park, NY: New City Press, 2012).

seem to come from beyond all else that exists and thereby to be capable of embracing all that merely is. The flash of transcendence we glimpse in each person we know is the "something more" that makes each a unique and irreplaceable whole unto himself or herself. When we know persons we know how they are in themselves. Nothing tangible or quantifiable or describable can give us this sense of the other. It is only the other in himself or herself that can communicate it. In doing so they communicate what cannot be communicated, for no one can have the experience that another has. Yet we routinely overstep that boundary. We know one another as persons over and above all that is said, because each is capable of giving himself or herself. The part can contain the whole when the word or touch says more than can be said. It is the miracle of communication that sustains all forms of discourse between us. We do not have to prove the possibility of relating to others because to be a person is to already be in relation to other persons. Responsibility is not something we choose but something that chooses us.

Levinas emphasized the face of the other that draws me before I am even aware of myself. No preparation in advance can steel us for the rupture by which the other pierces our consciousness. However it does serve to affirm what we already intuited. None of us exists apart from the bonds that hold us, for we are continually affected by the presence of others who save us from the isolation that is darker than any black hole.

Transcendence as mutuality

Transcendence is what marks the person. Even when what is said is fairly modest we can intuit the other who says more than what they say. We recognize the other and in that mutual recognition understanding breaks through. Each has made space for the other and, in that miracle of communication, shared himself or herself. The case of Helen Keller's struggle to understand words is a great example of that openness to one another that underpins the possibility of language, for the one thing that her teacher, Anne Sullivan, could not convey is that words point to something other than themselves.[19] We can point to everything in the world, but we cannot point to pointing as such. It is the elementary practice by which mothers communicate with babies, engaging in repetitive and imitative games that seem to have no purpose, until the smile of recognition breaks through. Yes, it is a moment of insight, but it is more than a grasp of things shared between them. It is a flash of mutuality by which otherness overflows all that is said and done. "It is with the heart," declared the Little Prince, "that one sees rightly." This is the way of heart knowledge that exceeds all of the information that may have been conveyed. Aristotle was the first to identify it as the highpoint of friendship he called joint attention, *sunaisthesis*, where in being conscious of something each of us is conscious of the other as also being conscious of it

19   *The Story of My Life by Helen Keller* (1902), Ch. IV. You can find the "water scene" in the famous movie from 1962, *The Miracle Worker*.

(*Nicomachean Ethics*, 1170b1–14).[20] In this culminating moment of sharing, the individual awareness that each possesses is intensified. Aristotle explained that this was why we want to spend time with our friends, for it is the apex of our own existence and of the existence of the other. By mutuality we become more than we could be in isolation.

Some of the drama of that climactic irruption is vividly on display in the description

20 "Now as we saw, his existence is desirable because he perceives his own goodness, and this kind of perception is in itself pleasant. Consequently he must also include his friend's existence in his consciousness (*sunaisthesthai hoti estin*), and that may be accomplished by living together with him and by sharing each other's words and thoughts. For this would seem to be what living together means when said of human beings: it does not mean feeding in the same place as it does in the case of cattle." [What translation? *Nicomachean Ethics*, trans. Martin Ostwald (Indianapolis: Bobbs-Merrill, 1962). See the excellent treatment of this idea in John von Heyking, *The Form of Politics: Plato and Aristotle on Friendship* (Toronto: McGill-Queens University Press, 2016).]

that Helen Keller gives of the moment when she finally understood that "w-a-t-e-r" meant that cool liquid pouring through her fingers as the well was being pumped. The eureka character of the event arises from the super-abundance that overflows it all. It is not just that she understood the word for water but that she understood words as such. The vast-ness of language and communication opened for her in a way that finally liberated her from the confines of what she could feel and touch in her immediate world. Released from the limits of time and space, Helen entered the world of persons that is the world of mean-ing. Wittgenstein made the same point in de-claring that a private language is impossible, for words inextricably connect us to a world of interpersonal relations. Yet no account of language can adequately explain that possi-bility to us. The unique journey that Helen had to undertake, after she was afflicted by blindness and deafness as an infant, meant that that the process had to follow a long and painful struggle. Her breakthrough was in the recognition of what signs and letters meant for someone else. It was in the sharing of awareness that the meaning of meaning became apparent. By knowing what it means for you I begin to glimpse what it means for me. The epiphany of joint attention discloses the transcendence that is the reality of the person. Each can set itself aside for the sake of including the other. As Helen Keller shows, it is the point at which words fail us but it also is what underpins the possibility of words, as well as the possibility of love that vastly exceeds what they say. This is why we can understand one another across all the barriers that separate us. We do not even need to be beside one another for that leap of understanding to occur. It is enough that we know one another inwardly, as mutual inwardnesses. It is not necessary for small babies to be able to speak for communication to occur. Even nonverbally, and certainly nondiscursively, the glimpse of otherness breaks through.

Without saying, everything is said. All saying arises from the person who is prior to all that is conveyed. Yielding place to the other, the very basis for the possibility of joint attention, can occur only because it has already occurred in the transcendence of the person. It would never be possible for a person to give himself or herself, to sacrifice the self or die for another, if that were not the possibility of the person from the beginning. This is surely what makes persons so difficult to plumb. Each is an unfathomable mode of being. Everything else we know is solidly in being as a continuing entity and strives mightily to retain its grasp on existence, but the person carries existence far more lightly and seems less tightly welded to it. Therein is the promise of love that every person carries, as the inwardness ever ready to include the inwardness of the other by setting itself aside. What kind of a being is so indifferent to being that it can yield place at so slight an invitation? What has happened to the putative struggle for survival that biology and politics lecture us about? The question itself suggests its own overturning, for it gives priority to truth over mere worldly satisfaction. But that still does not furnish us with a paradigm by which we might grasp the nature of the person, who seems to continually set aside all purely naturalistic drives.

Attainment of an answer to that question has occupied Western philosophy ever since it received its impetus in Socrates, who was prepared to die rather than abandon his testament to truth. It is one thing to behold the epiphany of self-transcendence, but it is something else to account for its condition of possibility. The closest we come to it is in the great spiritual traditions that attest in one way or another to the spark or the image of divinity within every one of us. In encountering the transcendent reality of God these traditions inevitably shed light on our capacity to receive the revelation. But the figurative language of images or sparks does not quite identify what it is that we share with the God who is beyond all. Instead, theological insights are often content to remain within the pictorial forms in which they first become expressed. They are more occupied with preservation of the canons they have received. The philosophical problems of their theophanies, however, remain. And we are eventually compelled to confront them unless we wish to find ourselves in the uncomfortable position of retelling sacred stories without being able to account for that possibility.

To be freed we must be touched by others who give far more than the hand by which they reach us. It is through the sharing of ourselves with others that we too exceed what we could become on our own. Even our thinking, as Aristotle noted, is deepened and intensified when it is in the company of friends. Left alone we cannot do as well, for it is only in company with others that what we think about becomes real and we ourselves become real. This is the difference that joint attention (*sunaisthesis*) makes. It is the promise of the shared story between us. In this way we go beyond the narratives that are shared and exchanged. To recollect what is of ultimate concern is to go beyond the accounts to the mutuality of those who undertake it. Sharing is the promise of friendship as both the condition and its fulfillment. Over and above the different traditions are the persons who bear them. They can share them because they are always more than and prior to the stories that are shared. That is the condition of possibility for our dialogue, as well as the end toward which it draws. Sharing carries within it the promise of a mutual self-giving that affirms what each person recounts in their respective modes. But that means that the fruit of the dialogue amounts to more than the respectful distance strangers and porcupines preserve between one another. The possibility of the unexpected hovers on the horizon of the conversation. Indeed the conversation is itself the first fruit of a hitherto unexpected enlargement of our horizons. The sharing of sacred story is not itself a sacred story, nor does it furnish a joint communiqué of agreement. It is itself the opening of community beyond the individual communities of the respective traditions.

To think about it we must invoke the idea of a universal humanity intimated within every historical revelation of the sacred yet never identical with any one of them. The spiritual message in every instance is universal, but it exists within its particular historical expression. To grasp the universal significance toward which they separately point we must open ourselves to all others who approach us from their respectively different viewpoints. The particulars that separate us are not abolished, but they are overcome by the mutuality that is our universal openness to one another. Nothing intervenes to block the openness of person to person.[21] The leap of understanding has occurred before anything has even been said. In this way we see that the universality of spiritual traditions is not just the end point of their sharing but the premise that underpins its possibility. Truth is not simply their goal but the mode of their existence. Its touchstone is the openness that seals a conversation already immunized against the possibility of untruth. Persons can meet only in the transcendence that is the meeting of persons. Universal humanity is glimpsed in the sharing by which differences are submerged in the mutuality of persons that remain beyond them. Just as persons are beyond what they say, separation is ever

---

21   "I am human and consider nothing human is alien to me." Terence (170 BC). Such a conversation is marvelously sketched in Jean Bodin's famous *Heptaplomeres or Colloquium of the Seven about the Secrets of the Sublime.*

subsumed within the recognition of unity. Humanity, or universal humanity, may be an eschatological index, never present in finite historical circumstance, but its recognition remains the province of very specific human beings as they go beyond themselves towards others. Only persons can grasp their own transcendental openness, because they live it as the medium of their existence.

As the ones who share their stories, persons lie beyond all that they share. This is the condition of possibility of their conversation. Mutuality precedes communication. It was this realization that underpinned the modern recognition of tolerance as the primary acknowledgment of our relationship to one another. Reverencing one another takes precedence over what we reverence separately. The realization struck John Locke so profoundly that he opened his famous *Letter on Toleration* (1689) with the assertion that he held tolerance to be "the mark of the true church." The principal consideration, he went on to explain, is that faith cannot be coerced because nothing can supplant the free assent that only the person himself or herself can give. In accepting or refusing, the person exceeds the boundaries of his or her action. Transcendence is invoked in a way that concretely outweighs all else in existence. Not even the divine command can dispense with that primordial freedom of the person. Religious or political authorities may seek to dispense with the inconvenience of individual conscience, but that is not how the divine voice itself issues its invitation to the human heart. The imperative of preserving that inviolability, however, becomes abundantly clear when we enter upon the conversation in which genuine sharing of story comes about. Then we begin to sense that we are always more than we may say or hold or profess. Persons in conversation continually exceed the content of what is said. We do not need to adduce something hidden or mystical to account for this. Nor is there an abstract or universal requirement governing the exchange. In every case the mutuality of persons arises out of the sharing of selves that are prior to all else that is shared. This is the condition of possibility announced in every meeting of persons as the core of what transpires between them.

The transcendence of persons may be elusive, but it is not subjective. Nothing is more real than the persons we know, even if they cannot be subsumed within the external aspects of their lives. We know them in themselves, not in what is visible about them. This is the source of their priority. They are not what they present to us. Even the face is not the other, although it is in the face that we gaze upon him or her. Like the mask (*prósōpon*) of the actor in Greek drama, the visible sign is only temporary, for the actor will assume other roles and present other sides to us, but the one who presents endures invisibly. Even when the character dies in the action, the one who portrays it does not. There is something of that inextinguishability about the person. A mystery remains. Even a world that does not handle the notion of mystery very well, a world that wants to measure all that is, cannot shake this primary experience of immeasurability that is each person we know. To name it "transcendence" may suggest a trail of ineffability, but that is hardly how we encounter the persons who matter most to us. They are the most definable reality of our lives. We know each one as a whole world in himself or herself. Far from relating on the surface level, they call forth a response that exceeds all else that is. It is in giving and receiving one another that we realize that persons are utterly beyond the finite boundaries within which they appear to us. In that epiphany we behold a substantive reality that surpasses all finite accounting. We do not live in space and time with all the chronometers we apply to those dimensions, but within a whole other order of being measured in personal giving. It can only be accessed by the opening that is unconditional. Love is stronger than death. We cannot love a person only in part, or for a while, or up to a certain limit. Who each one is can be seen only in light of the transcendence that each is and in the transcendence each calls forth in me.

The language of substance must be replaced by the language of relation. Therein lies the paradox of the person, for in giving ourselves we gain more than we have lost. It is the peculiarity of the person, of that which is spiritual, that it does not live by the laws of material existence. Transcendence is the reality of persons. They do not lose themselves in surrendering themselves. It can seem that the characterization of the person as pure relation undercuts the possibility of continuing identity by which the renunciation of self can take place. But that is always to assimilate persons to the world of things. Instead we must be prepared to think more deeply about the challenge that persons pose for our solidly material model of life. Nothing in the law of the jungle, the struggle for survival, prepares us for the unbidden acts of generosity that astonish us. Giving without calculation of return seems not to fit the zero-sum reality of kill or be killed. Yet people do throw themselves in front of buses to save strangers. They do not choose death but put themselves in place of the other. We say they have sacrificed themselves, but that is only to sidestep the mystery. How do they do it? How do they undertake an action that will certainly result in their death? Nothing provides a model except the astonishing reality of persons. We realize that they were never simply present in that substantial identity by which we knew them familiarly. Having beheld it they transcended it. In this way they could give their lives for another, even at the cost of their own. It was not that they one day entered another mode of being we call self-transcendence, but that they already lived within it right up to the moment when they disclosed it to themselves and us. The substance that can give its substance away has long departed from the world for which survival at any cost is the measure.

A "Puckish" Response to Walsh's Philosophy of the Person

Matthew D. Walz

The following is a slightly edited version of the remarks offered by Matthew Walz in response to David Walsh's lecture, "Person Means Relation."

Thank you, Professor Walsh, for your trenchant reflections on the person, in which at numerous moments you were marvelously pithy. I hope my response does justice to your reflections and paves the way toward a constructive dialogue regarding the human person.

When I undertook the happy task of reading Professor Walsh's lecture to prepare a response, I found myself pausing on multiple occasions to digest an especially concise and penetrating turn of phrase that provided a key insight into personhood. Professor Walsh's lecture is replete with several aphoristic kernels of wisdom about the person that gave me pause to wonder. Please indulge me as I recall a few of my favorites:

> The difficulty that he and we have is that we lack a means of visualizing what it means to be the kind of being that gives its being away.

> To be a person is to be like God who could hold onto his being, but out of love continually dispenses it.

> The end of a metaphysics of presence is palpable when it opens upon that which makes all presence possible.

> Only in a world of persons does it make sense to say that you become more by becoming less.

> It is in the logic of what it means to be a person that loss is gain, an experience that overwhelms every young mother with the astonishment of being the first to discover it.

The only way that persons can be known is personally. Over and above all that is said and done there is the person who is over and above all that is said and done.

The person, who had for so long been casually identified with the mask, now steps forward as its bearer. But of course there is nothing to see beyond the self-presentation that has been made. The person remains invisible even to themselves. Inwardness is an elusive medium.

Cruelty is impossible when we look on the face of the other as the face of inwardness.

In the end the only model of the person is Jesus Christ and those who find their substance on the far side of loss.

We can question the goal or the end of history because we always already stand beyond it. The person is the apocalypse of history.

What kind of a being is so indifferent to being that it can yield place at so slight an invitation? What has happened to the putative struggle for survival that biology and politics have lectured us about? Even the question itself suggests its own overturning, for it gives priority to truth over mere worldly satisfaction.

Reverencing one another takes precedence over what we reverence separately.

Nothing in the law of the jungle, the struggle for survival, prepares us for the unbidden acts of generosity that astonish us. Giving without calculation of return seems not to fit the zero-sum reality of kill or be killed. Yet people do throw themselves in front of a bus to save a stranger. They do not choose death, but put themselves in place of the other.

The substance that can give its substance away has long departed from the world for which survival at any cost is the measure.

I had to be selective here; for there were many other poignant assertions that I could have added to this list. Like the ones I just read, each of them too would encapsulate a keen, concisely articulated insight provided by someone who has pondered deeply the marvelous mystery of the person. And so, again, first and foremost, I thank our Aquinas Lecturer for sharing with us the fruits of his contemplation of personhood.

The compelling thread that runs through Professor Walsh's lecture is the search for a model to understand the "super-reality" of persons in comparison to things, a model to understand the reality of extraordinary "someones" in comparison to ordinary "some-things." Taking a cue from Thomas Aquinas's theological articulation of the person, Professor Walsh suggests that the search for a model to understand the person goes astray when-ever one deploys a model "from below," as it were, rather than "from above." To be under-stood adequately, in other words, a person has to be encountered directly, in his or her own right, at his or her own level; and ultimately the fullness of a person's reality can be illumi-nated only in light of our eminently personal and essentially relational God.

With the help of these persuasive claims of Professor Walsh, we are set free to imagine re-ality—all of reality, from top to bottom—as thoroughly *personalized* and, thus, as thor-oughly *relational*, both internally and externally. Every reality, then, is either a person or ought to be understood in relation to the person, es-pecially the Creator-Person who personally chose that each being exist as some sort of likeness of himself.

It is fascinating to me what comes to light when we gaze upon reality through this fully personalized lens, even when we are gazing upon those things—animals, plants, non-living things—that do not in fact occupy the status of persons. To my mind, at least, someone who has captured this precisely and beautifully is Gerard Manley Hopkins, the great English poet and Jesuit priest. I think, for example, of his poem "As kingfishers catch fire," and the following lines in particular:

> Each mortal thing does one thing and the same:
>   Deals out that being indoors each one dwells;
> Selves—goes its self; *myself* it speaks and spells,
>   Crying *What I do is me: for that I came.*

And so my initial reaction to Professor Walsh's lecture is: "Yes! True! Right on! Persons are . . . indeed . . . PERSONS!"

But then the "old man" in me, the curmudgeonly Aristotelian, begins to manifest himself. "Hey, wait a second, are persons really that different, really that far out of reach, philosophically speaking? Is there a way to reel them in, to capture them somehow in terms of substance, in terms of a 'metaphysics of presence'?" And thus I find myself in a quandary. Interiorly, I find myself caught in the crossfire of an ongoing argument between the "personalist" or "philosopher of the person," on the one hand, and the stubborn "Aristotelian" or "philosopher of substance," on the other.

And so I wonder: Does Professor Walsh experience this same interior struggle? I ask him this not with a view to putting our Aquinas Lecturer on the spot. I intend the question, rather, as an opportunity for him to help us figure out how exactly to wed a personalistic approach to human persons with a metaphysical approach like that of Aristotle, who seems fairly intent on making sure that our reflections on the human being, especially in an ethical and political light, never become too untethered from the reality of our materiality, our physicality, our being part of a world in which loss is in fact loss and gain is in fact gain—a world that really is framed, at least in part, by the "struggle for survival that biology and politics have lectured us about," a world in which we really do aim for "worldly satisfaction."

To flesh out my quandary a bit more, it may be helpful to think of it as a kind of struggle between my inner Miranda (from Shakespeare's *Tempest*) and my inner Puck (from his *Midsummer Night's Dream*). One side of my brain—undoubtedly the right side!—proclaims with Miranda: "Oh, wonder! / How many goodly creatures are there here! / How beauteous mankind is! O brave new world / That has such [persons] in 't!" (V.1.215–18). But the other side of my brain—the left side, then?—jestingly grumbles with Puck: "Shall we their fond pageant see? / Lord, what fools these mortals be!" (III.2.116–17).

Perhaps, then, I can rephrase my question for Professor Walsh thus: How does a proper encounter with human persons and an adequate understanding of them digest and assimilate this Puckish, Aristotelian perception of the apparently inescapable finite and fatiguing condition of human existence?

Indeed, even the mother whom you mentioned in your lecture—who, like Miranda, is astonished at her beauteous newborn child—must nonetheless work, seemingly non-stop, in order to keep alive this fragile, needy animal to whom she gave birth. Furthermore, many of our political struggles seem connected with this quandary. I am thinking, for example, of how society accepts or fails to accept those whose limitations or special needs cover over or truncate some of their capacities to express their full personhood. I think, too, of the unborn, whose personhood is not altogether manifest and who, therefore, are at great risk of being treated as non-persons.

This, then, is my ongoing quandary, my ongoing struggle, with a philosophy—and, maybe even more so, with a *politics*—of the person. Can a Miranda-like vision of persons be grounded sufficiently in the natural parameters of a Puckish world in which mortality seems very real, in which the personhood of persons is often not very evident, and in which loss seems to be . . . well, just that: mere loss?

Thank you, again, Professor Walsh, for your stimulating lecture. I hope that the questions that I've raised, as well as the questions that those in the audience will raise in just a few minutes, provide further opportunities for you to share with us more of your timely insights concerning the person.

RESPONSE TO
PROFESSOR WALZ

I am deeply indebted to Matt Walz for his perceptive reading of my text. It is gratifying to have a reader who follows one's argument with such sympathy and yet does not flinch from addressing the reservations that remain. I am grateful too for the opportunity to develop a response, since I know that the misgivings expressed are likely to be shared by others. It is for this reason that I welcome Professor Walz as a dialogue partner who in every respect exemplifies the major claim of the text: that we think better in the company of friends than we would alone. This is by no means an original insight but one that is most prominently invoked by Aristotle. But like many things in Aristotle, it is more often bypassed when it should stop us from passing by. Typically viewed as a nostrum that makes sense in a general way, we overlook the potential for a deeper reading of his suggestion. To do so would confront us with a fundamental challenge to the way we routinely think about the life of mind and thus the life of persons. Just because we are physically alone in our study does not mean we are actually alone. We are instead immersed in a rich conversation with others, indeed many others, who are the silent and invisible partners of a dialogue that extends well beyond our own consciousness. It is impossible to think without measuring our thoughts in relation to the thinking of others. For this reason, I am doubly gratefully for Professor Walz's willingness to become an audible and visible partner in our joint conversation.

I mention this not only by way of a polite preliminary to the exchange but one that hits upon the very core of the concerns that are raised within it. That is, that the philosophical language we have inherited from the classic sources is not always adequate, not only to what we want to say but what they too intended to say. It is a great mistake to assume that terminology can be taken over even from a genius as formidable as Aristotle without further examination. But it is also a mistake to think that any revision necessarily involves a departure from what they have given us. Modern philosophy itself has so often understood itself in opposition to the classics that the claim has been taken at face value without the scrutiny it deserves. What if there really is no such opposition but an underlying continuity that masks a deeper unity? How indeed can there be a history of philosophy without that inner affinity? Such intuitions are familiar once we begin the study of specific thinkers, but they are hard to voice within an intellectual framework strongly predisposed to the split between ancients and moderns. That disjunction seems so much a part of our intellectual furniture that we seem incapable of conceiving of things in any other way. This is why it is so important to go back to Aristotle himself to interrogate the categories he left us with a view to the possibility that they never really possessed the fixity he seemed to assign them. The very comprehensiveness of a systematic thinker like Aristotle deflects our attention from the ways in which reality does not quite fit as neatly as it is presented within his account. Admirers in particular have been prone to overlook the ways in which Aristotle too was less than satisfied with his own resolution of problems.

We might even suggest that the greatness of Aristotle consists in his unwillingness to disguise the tensions and conflicts that remain within his thought. They become apparent to all fair readers, for he seems to be continually coming up against dead ends that he flatly acknowledges. He cannot, for example, find an answer to the question as to how it is possible to persuade those who display little interest in acting nobly that that is precisely where their own true good lies (1114b5ff). After noting the importance of a good upbringing for those who want to discuss such questions, he returns over and over again to the frank admission that it is impossible to instill a desire for nobility in those who declare their indifference to it. What should one do, we are inclined to ask, if it is precisely our responsibility to inculcate the good upbringing Aristotle has conveniently stipulated as a prerequisite? Again, he touches on virtually the same issue when he contemplates the weak-willed or incontinent man who has not so much chosen self-indulgence as failed to save himself from it (Book VII). How is it that he has been unable to see what is so plain to the man of practical wisdom, that right action must become the norm and measure of a whole life? That without virtue he cannot even see the good for which he wishes and at which he aims? It may be fine for Aristotle to hold up the model of the magnanimous man (*megalapsychos*) or the mature man (*spoudaios*) as the paradigm to be emulated, but how does one arrive at the conviction that one must become the measure of what is highest and best in the moral life? If one were to dwell for long on these existential questions one would realize that we have left behind the neatly structured account of ends and virtues, the teleological framework of happiness announced at the beginning of the *Nicomachean Ethics*. Apart from those who are capable of sustaining the inner formation of character, there seem to be many lost souls on the periphery who are incapable of sustaining the necessary rigors. To consign them to the supervision of the legislator, those for whom coercion must replace the role of persuasion in the *Politics*, is perhaps not so satisfactory an outcome as the suggestion initially appeared.

For one thing there is the very large question as to how these different human types can form a *polis*, a *politeia* of sharing and of friendship, when the gulf between them yawns so large. The point, however, is not to take a cheap shot at Aristotle but to suggest that the conventional reading of his account of virtue ethics, solidly grounded in a stable account of human nature, is more problematic than is usually conceded. In short, Aristotle was no Aristotelian. He knew that outside of his own core analysis lay an untidy penumbra in which what it meant to be a human being discovering and disclosing who one is, was more mysterious than anticipated. Without using the term person, *prosopon*, he comes very close to Pirandello's famous title of *Six characters in search of an author*. We recall too that his own work on the *Poetics* has not always been read in close relationship with his *Ethics*. In other words, even in Aristotle, the ostensible author of a substance-based metaphysics, we seem never to be far from the sense that reality is continually disclosed through action rather than through contemplation. The difficulty is that the self-characterization of his noetic science as *theoria* suggests a detachment regarding things that are primarily glimpsed through participation within them. All of these tensions are familiar to scholars of Aristotle, who can point out numerous other irreconcilables within his thought. Unfortunately, such scholars tend to remain at that level of general observation, presuming they must refrain from following the master into regions to which he points without explicitly entering. Surely to be a conscientious Aristotelian would entail a pursuit of the adventure beyond where Aristotle has taken it! It would thereby become more faithful to his inspiration than any mere following of the words. We recall that the text arises from life and narrates more than it says. It is the work of a person and can be read only by persons who are prepared to assume responsibility for its further unfolding.

The dialectical process of Aristotle's thought is in every respect the living reality of a mind in motion; contemplation remains for him an activity, as he continually emphasized, rather than a mode of rest. Plato, by contrast, benefited from a more thoroughly inter-personalist mode of inquiry and presentation because he wrote almost exclusively in the form of dialogues where the *dramatis personae* exemplified the dialectic of thinking. We often forget the extent to which the classic texts are themselves an ongoing conversation with readers who span the centuries and continue to enroll us too in the communities of mutual exchange that they actually founded. In this respect they are hardly different from the gospels that are not so much a record of past events as a living invitation to enter again into their meaning in the present. The Church, while it may make use of historical scholarship, does not confuse that with the reading of the word that occurs in every liturgy. All is geared not toward an eyewitness report, but toward the encounter that unfolds inwardly as each of us confronts the question the text itself raises. "Who do

you say that I am?" We have become participants in the dialog, often without suspecting
it and initially with only the barest intuition
of what its burden might entail. This is evident if we recall the opening of the *Republic*
that seems to be an account of what happened yesterday, until we recall that there
can be no such report unless there is a recip-
ient. The primary interlocuter of Socrates is
the reader. The Good may be the central axis
toward which the account marches, but how
is it to be glimpsed? Despite all the stall tac-
tics and all of the misgivings employed along
the way, it can only be attained when one
person begins to discern what is beheld inwardly by another. How else would it be
possible to convey the central thought of the
dialogue? That is, that the Good is not an
idea that can be grasped and transmitted
from one person to another, but the very condition of possibility of the dialogue itself. It
is, Socrates declares enigmatically, that
which gives the power of knowing to those
who know and the power of being known to
that which is known (*Republic* 508e). As the
horizon within which the whole exchange

has unfolded it is about as far away from a substance that is present as it is possible to be.

The truth about being may remain the focus of the dialogue, especially in the central discussion of the philosopher-king, but the difficulty of conveying it is continually heightened. We are reminded that the central political challenge is to convince those who are not philosophers that they ought to follow the lead of the one who is. The unsatisfactory nature of the exchange is derived from this insuperable barrier that remains a permanent feature of every human community marked by the diversity of types that compose it. It is the same diversity as pervades the dialogue itself and thus what justifies the self-designation of their conversation as a "city in speech." Their dialogue replicates what they are talking about. But this means that there is a wide spectrum of understanding by which the respective partners grasp the project of their discourse. At the most minimal level they must discuss something external to their conversation as if it exists somewhere else. But what could be more real than that which makes it possible for them to apprehend the object of their discourse? Yet that is inevitably the procedure they must follow when not all can see that they already inhabit that city in talking about it. If it is real then it must exist somewhere and if it is not in the historical Athens toward which the nocturnal exchange is directed then it must be somewhere else. From this derives the notion that it exists as an *eidos* or form of the city laid up in the heavens for those who wish to contemplate it and realize it within the actual community. It is in this way that a note of pseudo-objectivity enters into the conversation. If the *kallipolis* is the true city then it is somewhere else other than the glimpse shared by the conversation partners, for they lack a way of grasping the truth as the condition of their exchange itself. This is the limitation imposed by the presence of non-philosophic partners. They cannot see what cannot be presented in a non-pictorial fashion. Hence they cling to, and philosophy itself remains linked to, a figurative style of discourse that is belied by the nature of the conversation itself.

In truth, the city in speech exists nowhere but in truth itself. Even Plato seems to have conceded the elusiveness of what is realized most piercingly only between the dialogue partners, for whom the intensiveness of the inquiry furnished the principal access they had to the truth that was the condition of its possibility. What makes the *Republic* the towering literary achievement it is is that it is one of the few dialogues where the author too manages to reach beyond the limits of what at bottom remains a discursive exchange. By invoking the language of paradox he has been able to say what cannot so easily be said directly. Words have been made to say what remains beyond them, because it hovers perpetually at the boundary of the conversation. It is arguable that this entails the risk of the interlocuters not being able to follow what is said, a risk that is more than literary for it portends the breakdown of the political community that is being constituted. It was a risk that Plato tended not run in any of the succeeding dialogues and the principal reason for the impression that those later works are marked

by a literary decline, at least from the pene-
tration that is reached in the *Republic*. What
makes the breakthrough possible here is the
presence of Glaucon and Adeimantus who,
if they are not philosophic minds, at least
possess the radical openness to truth that
would eventually transform them into such,
if they submit completely to their calling.
Even if they have not yet made the response,
they are capable of it and thus can hear the
call.

Elsewhere (in the Seventh Letter) Plato
more explicitly remarks on the impossibility of transmitting the truth of philosophy
in the form of a result that can be written
down. Instead, he explains, it is more in the
manner of a spark or an inspiration that
leaps from one soul to another as the
means by which it catches fire. But in the
Republic it is notable that he does not even
exclude the non-philosophic types from
catching a glimpse of what is more fully
gazed upon in that culminating revelation
of the Good. All men possess the capacity
for gazing on the brightest part of being,
even those who have resolutely turned

their backs upon it.[1] They have not quite been able to suppress an awareness of what it is that has called them and against which they have turned their faces. This is what makes the philosopher an authority within the city, for he is distinguished only by seeing and hearing the truth that is seen and heard, even in its rejection, by all others. The city may be hierarchically structured, but it is an order that is rooted in a common recognition of the justice that binds all of them and none more com-

---

1   "If this is true, then, we must conclude that education is not what it is said to be by some, who profess to put knowledge into a soul which does not possess it, . . . On the contrary, our own account signifies that the soul of every man does possess the power of learning the truth and the organ to see it with; and that, just as one might have to turn the whole body round in order that the eye should see light instead of darkness, so the entire soul must be turned away from this changing world, until its eye can bear to contemplate reality and that supreme splendor which we have called the Good." *Republic*, trans. Francis Cornford (Oxford: Oxford University Press, 1941), Book VII, 518.

pletely than the person whose insight grasps it most completely. From there they derive the notion of what is "right by nature," the foundation of an appeal to nature as a criterion of right that reigns in splendid isolation above the varying opinions men hold to excuse and justify the disorder of their lives. Not everyone is touched by the unseen measure that emerges when nature becomes transparent for an order beyond itself, for the philosophic discovery has not abolished the plurality of the human responses to it. Even among the students of Socrates there could always arise an Alcibiades who was spiritually sensitive enough to confess the pull of the golden chord, yet sufficiently resistant to it that he refused to respond.[2] Even the later specifications of *koinai ennoiai*, common opinions, and a natural law, scarcely managed to do more than furnish a misplaced sense of concreteness where none existed. Truth, the truth of order, could not assume a definition that would

2   Plato, *Symposium*.

render obsolete the need for a personal appropriation.

The requirement for conversion, the Alcibiades problem, could not be avoided. The truth of being, substance, could not be apprehended in any other way. If we take this as the centerpiece of Platonic-Aristotelian philosophy then we begin to see why, even in the absence of a developed account of the person, they inevitably operated with a sense of the person as engaged in a dynamic of self-enactment and self-disclosure. Right by nature, and the Good that is beyond being, can be grasped only by one who is neither a part of nature nor a substance but one whose character is inescapably tied to the existential choice that the souls in the underworld and in the Piraeus are compelled to make. In the end it is not simply by standing apart from the whole that the classic philosophers gained their deepest insights into it, for it was through their role as participants that the greatest illumination was vouchsafed to them. One thinks of Aristotle's elevation of the contemplative life as superior to the practical life while he simultaneously insists that contemplation is itself activity of the highest order. But it is when he deals with the prospect of an infinite regress in terms of final causes that we see how much his analysis turns on the experience of action, and thus of the acting person. The notion of a final cause as an ultimate *ad quem* is defended, not as a metaphysical necessity, an ultimate appeal to the notion of being or substance that a universe marked by efficient causality has irrevocably excluded, but as an imperative arising from human life itself. In other words, it is at that point where Aristotle wants to affirm the ultimacy of substance that he derives it from that least substantial of all foundations: the person who cannot live except in relation to what is beyond himself and who therefore reveals the extent to which he provides the principal access to an anchoring substance. Person as relation does not require a prior affirmation of substance for each is the one who is in attunement with what endures eternally. The passage in the *Metaphysics* where Aristotle explains why there cannot be an infinite regress is a precious opening on the interior source of his reflection. For "those who maintain the infinite series eliminate the Good without knowing it (yet no one would try to do anything if he were not going to come to a limit); nor would there be reason in the world; the reasonable man, at least, always acts for a purpose, and this is a limit; for the end is a limit."[3] Reason conscious of itself discloses the structure of reality more profoundly than any claim that might be made on behalf of being as a first principle. How else would Aristotle have had access to a notion of substance except by living within it? The one who remains true to truth testifies more compellingly than any principle of truth.

That conviction, however, does not rest on anything more unassailable than the self-realization of the one who carries it within. Concern with the notion of substance outside of the acting person, the person as relation, a concern to which Professor Walz legitimately

3   *Metaphysics* 994b8–16, trans. W. D. Ross, *The Basic Works of Aristotle*, ed. Richard McKeon (New York: Random House, 1941).

gives voice, remains valid. Not surprisingly it was also a primary concern for Aristotle, as it was for Plato. What makes Aristotle's response so striking is that he went deeper into what we have termed interiority in order to emerge with the only reassurance that remains available to all of us who ask the same question. How can I hold as true what I hold only inwardly? Is it not preferable to hold onto the truth of substance even if that holding on is the effort of the person who has no other substance than that conviction itself? In short, is the perception of thinking as an event of ourselves alone correct or accurate? Again, the problem does not arise directly for Aristotle. It nowhere appears in his account of the soul, the *De Anima*, nor in the remarks on knowledge scattered throughout his writings. As with the account of final causes in the *Metaphysics*, the social construction of knowledge, as we might call it, emerges most surprisingly in the analysis of friendship in Book IX of the *Ethics*. Within a masterful and comprehensive account of human relationships, under the heading of friendship we are treated to a systematic reflection on associational life that ranges from the transactional, to the superficial, to the most intimate, that seems to lead the author himself into depths he had not previously plumbed. Beyond the obvious observations that friends are characterized by the sharing of their likes and dislikes, made most evident by their desire and practice of spending time together, there is the growing awareness that what they most share is the bond of friendship, *philia*, that makes them dear to one another. Without employing the language of interiority, Aristotle reflects on the extent to which they give themselves to and for one another. By spending money on behalf of the friend one partner gains material benefits while the other acquires nobility. Each comes to regard the other as another self, a striking expression that alerts us to the degree to which Aristotle has opened the path to inwardness that is the true realm of friendship (*Ethics* 1166a30ff). What St. Thomas discovers in his remarkable formulation that the person means relation is powerfully evident in the Aristotelian analysis as a form of self-giving that becomes the innermost mark of every human association.

Yet that innermost bond, by which each sets himself aside for the sake of the other, has no other reality than the moment of inwardness through which it emerges. This was the remarkable breakthrough that Aristotle reached as he dug deeper into what makes friendship possible. He sought to explain what it is like to be friends from within the relationship, just what exceeds the horizon of the durability of substance. It reaches what is more lasting than substance because it has already yielded place to it and thereby arrived at the substance that is beyond loss. This is the apex of thinking that can scarcely be thought unless it is somehow glimpsed in the mind of an other. This was the point at which the breakthrough to transcendence could finally acquire the kind of stability at which the language of substance aims. It is what is real. But where is that reality and how is it glimpsed? The answer for Aristotle was that it was in the event of *sunaisthesis*, a neologism he seems to have coined to express that remarkable moment when persons experience their joint perception or joint attention on what matters most to them. It is "to share in a friend's awareness that he is (*sunaisthesthai hoti estin*), and this would come through living together and sharing conversation and thinking; for this would seem to be what living together means in the case of human beings (*Nicomachean Ethics*, 1170b10–12)."[4] To demonstrate that this was not a passing aside but somehow central to the whole topic of what friendship means, Aristotle went on to explain that this is why good men desire friends. While not needing friends for the sake of utility and scarcely for the sake of pleasure, they cannot do without them for the practice of virtue in the good life. It is by sharing one another's thoughts and words that friendship is constituted, rather than "feeding in the same place as it does with cattle."

Mutuality is what heightens and intensifies the consciousness that each of us possesses in isolation. This is why Aristotle emphasizes the role of friendship in the good life. Left to ourselves we are incapable of

4   *Nicomachean Ethics*, trans. Martin Ostwald (Indianapolis: Bobbs-Merrill, 1962).

thinking and acting continuously, but in the company of others we are lifted beyond ourselves and reach up toward the friendship of the gods by which we lead a life beyond the human (Bk.X, ch.7). Friendship, person as relation, has become even for Aristotle the model of reality even though he lacks the means of fully articulating it. The concern that this introduces a note of indeterminacy into the account, while it is one whose validity Aristotle recognizes, is ultimately one he rejects. He counsels against those who insist that we are human beings who must remain within the limits of what is possible for human beings. Instead he holds out the prospect of reaching beyond the human level "to become immortal as far as that is possible and do our utmost to live in accordance with what is highest in us. For though this is a small portion (of our nature), it far surpasses everything else in power and value. One might even regard it as each man's true self, since it is the controlling and better part (1177b35–1178a3)." The true self that both Aristotle and Plato discovered surpasses what merely is in the order of being, for it invites us to go beyond who we are. The discovery of the person as relation as the transcendence of self is on the horizon even before that language has been differentiated. It would take the Christian discovery of *metanoia*, the conversion of the old man into the new man that Christ has made visible, for the dynamic of what it means to be a person to become evident. Holding a mask and playing a role was certainly a perspective available to the Greeks, but it was not yet possible to recognize that philosophy itself was already engaged in the movement by which a person becomes other than he is. The practice was well ahead of the theory available to describe it, including the singular initiative of grace or gift as the invitation that opens each person toward the discovery of who he or she is. The friendship between God and man that was incomprehensible to Aristotle would eventually be comprehended in the surpassing action by which God becomes man.

When God puts himself in place of man, the fixity of substance is overturned. Now we glimpse the possibility of man becoming God in a way that is utterly beyond the hesitant speculations of Aristotle. Being as substance loses its primacy when it is replaced by the understanding of being as a person. Yet that does not render the previous account obsolete. What remains true remains truly within it. The difference is that it no longer retains the model of immanent being that had for so long been attached to it. Aristotle undoubtedly glimpsed this as he meditated on what it means for the discovery of the true self, the *nous* of a person, as a process of self-sacrifice on behalf of others. A breakthrough is marked when this is glimpsed as not simply the pattern of human *nous* but of the divine *Nous* itself. Now substance in the immanent sense can be set aside for the deeper revelation of *ousia* as a movement of self-transcendence that is personal through and through. Substance, that which endures through all changes, is no longer immanent being, but personal being that has already transcended and suffered on behalf of all. It is perhaps not too implausible to suggest that person is the model of substance rather than the other way around. Only that which contains its own being within itself, that which can freely give itself away, is what endures beyond all the vicissitudes of existence. Rather than thinking of self-transcendence as in danger of losing the substance that underpins, we might more properly think of self-transcendence as what make substance possible. It is for this reason that I derive great confidence from the example of St. Thomas who, when he came to think about substance in the highest sense, promptly declared both that person is the highest reality and that person means relation. Filling in the details as to how and what that means I take as the work of philosophy that stretches into our own time. I am grateful to my friends at the University of the Dallas for the kind invitation and the willingness to think together in one another's company. It is only because I cannot name all who made the visit such a memorable occasion that I must single out on their behalf our unparalleled host, Chris Mirus, and his assistant, Gema Guevara, as well as my genial and supportive conversation partner, Matt Walz, who along with my friends, Bill and Therese Frank, provided such warm hospitality. As a small mark of appreciation I dedicate this text to Bill and Therese with fond memories of times spent together.